DO ALL SPIDERS SPIN WEBS?

Questions and Answers About Spiders

BY MELVIN AND GILDA BERGER
ILLUSTRATED BY ROBERTO OSTI

CONTENTS

KEY TO ABBREVIATIONS
cm = centimeter/centimetre
ha = hectare
kg = kilogram
m = meter/metre
t = tonne

Text copyright © 2000 by Melvin Berger and Gilda Berger.
Illustrations copyright © 2000 by Roberto Osti.
All rights reserved. Published by Scholastic Inc.
SCHOLASTIC and associated logos are trademarks and/or registered trademarks of Scholastic Inc.

No part of this publication may be reproduced, or stored in a retrieval system, or transmitted in any form or by any means, electronic, mechanical, photocopying, recording, or otherwise, without written permission of the publisher. For information regarding permission, write to Scholastic Inc., Attention: Permissions Department, 555 Broadway, New York, NY 10012.

Library of Congress Cataloging-in-Publication Data

Berger, Melvin.
  Do all spiders spin webs? : questions and answers about spiders / by Melvin Berger and Gilda Berger; illustrated by Roberto Osti.
    p.   cm.—(Scholastic question & answer series)
  Includes index.
  Summary: Questions and answers present information about spiders, arranged in the categories "Amazing Creatures," "Web spinners," "Spiders that hunt" and "Living with Spiders."
  1. Spiders—Miscellanea—Juvenile literature. [1. Spiders—Miscellanea. 2. Questions and Answers.]
  I. Title. II. Berger, Gilda. III. Osti, Roberto, ill. IV. Series: Berger, Melvin. Scholastic question and answer series.
  QL458.4.B47 2000 595.4′4 21—dc21 99-042738 CIP AC

ISBN 0-439-09586-7 (pob); ISBN 0-439-14881-2 (pb)

Book design by David Saylor and Nancy Sabato

20 19 18 17 16 15 14 13   05 06 07 08 09

Printed in the U.S.A.   08
First trade printing, September 2000

Expert Reader: Don Moore, Wildlife Conservation Society, Central Park Wildlife Center, New York, NY

The spider on the front cover is a black widow spider. The spider on the title page is a trapdoor spider.

For Matthew, totally wonderful!
— M. AND G. BERGER

For my wife, Angela
— R. OSTI

INTRODUCTION

Lots of people are afraid of spiders. In fact, so many of us are frightened by spiders that there's a word for that fear—arachnophobia (uh-rak-nuh-FOH-be-uh).

You may or may not have arachnophobia. You may know that there is no reason to fear most spiders. And you may know that most spiders don't harm humans. In fact, you may even know that spiders are vital to our survival because they eat huge numbers of insects.

But did you know that

- all spiders have fangs and are poisonous?
- spider silk is stronger than a steel thread of the same thickness?
- some spiders eat frogs and birds, as well as insects?

The pictures and words of *Do All Spiders Spin Webs?* will give you a close-up look at the amazing world of spiders. You'll soon see for yourself the many ways spiders go about finding food and escaping their enemies. And you'll realize why spiders have survived on Earth for many, many millions of years!

AMAZING CREATURES

Do all spiders spin webs?

No. All spiders produce silk threads. But not all spiders spin webs.

Web-spinning spiders use the silk to spin webs that trap the flying or crawling insects that they feed on. Hunting spiders use their silk to help them catch insects and in other ways, too.

What kinds of webs do web spinners build?

All kinds. With their silk threads they build

- tangled webs with messy-looking threads that go this way and that;
- funnel webs on the ground with wide, mouthlike openings on top and the narrow part at the bottom;
- sheet webs above the ground that may be flat or shaped like hammocks or domes;
- orb webs with spokes like bicycle wheels;
- and many, many other web designs.

Do spiders get caught in their own webs?

Rarely. Spiders know their own webs. They stay away from the sticky silk threads that make up most of the web. Instead, they walk on the strands of dry silk.

Spiders also often coat their legs with an oily substance from their mouths. If a spider steps on a sticky thread, its oily feet keep it from getting caught.

Garden spider

Orb weaver

Sheet web spider

Grass spider

Social spiders

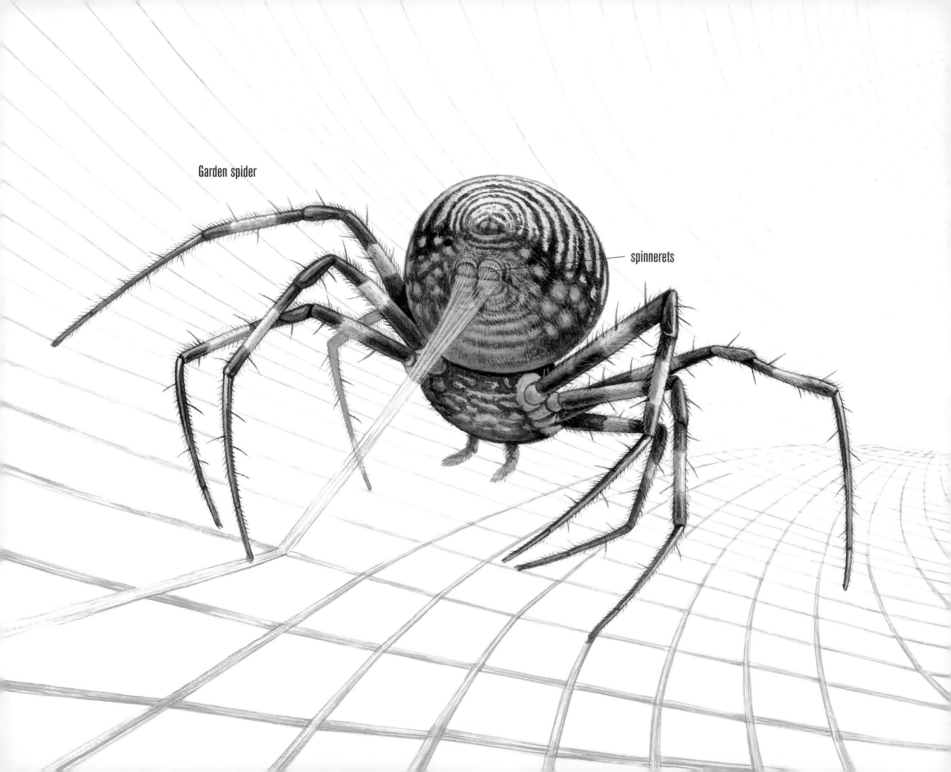

Garden spider

spinnerets

How else do spiders use their silk?

Almost all web spinners and hunters make draglines. These are long silk threads that trail behind the spiders as they move about. The spider attaches its dragline to a surface and uses it to drop down from a height or to make a giant leap to escape an enemy.

Spiders sometimes use silk to wrap their prey. Those that live in burrows, or tunnels, make silk linings for their nests. And females may weave silk sacs in which to lay their eggs.

How do spiders make silk?

With spinnerets at the rear end of their bodies. The spinnerets stick out like tiny fingers. Most spiders have six spinnerets, but some have two or four.

The spider forces a liquid out through the spinnerets. The liquid comes from its silk glands. As soon as the fluid hits the air, it hardens into a long, thin thread.

Spiders can spin different kinds of silk—thick or thin, sticky or dry, smooth or bumpy.

How strong is a spider's silk thread?

Very! In fact, spider silk is one of the strongest materials on Earth. A thread of silk is stronger than a steel thread of the same thickness. A rope of spider silk 1 inch (2.5 cm) thick could hold up a load of 74 tons (75 t). That's the weight of 50 automobiles!

Are spiders insects?

No. Spiders are arachnids (uh-RAK-nidz). Mites, ticks, and scorpions are other arachnids you may know. Count the hairy legs of any spider. You'll find there are eight. Insects, you may know, have only six legs.

Arachnids have two body parts, not three like adult insects. And spiders don't have wings or antennae (feelers) on their head like most insects. Also, newborn spiders look about the same as adults. Most newborn insects look very different from their parents.

Who first called spiders arachnids?

The ancient Greeks. According to legend, Arachne (uh-RAK-nee) was a skilled weaver of cloth. One day she challenged the goddess Athena to a weaving contest. Arachne won. This made Athena very angry, and she ordered that Arachne be hanged. At the last minute, however, Athena changed her mind. Instead of hanging Arachne, Athena turned her into a spider and forced her to spend the rest of her life spinning silk. And so, spiders became known as arachnids.

How many eyes do spiders have?

Usually eight, sometimes fewer. But how well they see is another story!

Spiders that spin webs have very poor eyesight. These spiders depend more on their sense of touch than on their good eyesight.

Many hunting spiders, on the other hand, have very good vision, which they need to spot and catch their prey.

Do spiders have ears?

No. But spiders have very good hearing. They pick up sound vibrations with tiny hairs on their legs and other parts of their bodies. Hunting spiders can pick up the softest sounds of bugs crawling or flying nearby.

Buzzing spiders

Do spiders make sounds?

Yes. But not with vocal cords as you do. When in danger, some bird-eating spiders produce a hissing sound by rubbing their front legs against their jaws. Male European buzzing spiders vibrate their bodies against leaves that have females on them. The vibration produces a buzzing sound, giving these spiders their name. And male wolf spiders drum on the ground with their front legs to attract mates.

How do spiders pick up odors?

With the same hairs on their bodies that pick up sound vibrations. Shave off a spider's hairs, and it can neither hear nor smell!

These remarkable hairs do even more. They give the spiders their sense of touch. Spiders can feel a puff of air so gentle that it stirs only one hair!

What color is a spider's blood?

Pale blue—not red like your blood. Also, the spider's blood doesn't flow through blood vessels. Instead it fills all the empty spaces within the spider's body.

The spider's blood also has the very important job of keeping the spider's legs stiff. If the spider loses too much blood, its legs curl up and it can't walk!

Do spiders breathe?

Indeed they do. Near the back of the body of most spiders is a small hole through which air enters. Tiny tubes on the inside carry the air to different parts of the body.

Other spiders have so-called book lungs. These are layers of tissue that look like 15 or more thin, flat pages of a book. Blood in these layers picks up oxygen from air that enters through slits in the body.

What do spiders eat?

Insects, mostly. If you could weigh all the insects that spiders eat in one year, they would weigh more than all the people on Earth!

Some spiders are cannibals and eat other spiders. Also, large spiders may eat small animals—birds, frogs and tadpoles, fish, and lizards.

How do spiders kill their prey?

They bite with their two sharp, poisonous fangs. The spider shoots the poison out through its fangs and into the insect.

The poison, which comes from glands within the spider's head, is strong enough to kill a small insect right away. It paralyzes larger animals and kills them more slowly.

Do spiders chew their food?

No. Spiders can't chew. They can only suck up liquids or foods that are soft or soupy. So, before a spider can swallow anything, it must first turn the food into a kind of mush.

After catching an insect, the spider injects saliva into the victim. The saliva turns the insect's solid flesh into a squishy pulp, which the spider then sucks up. All that the spider leaves behind is the insect's hard, crunchy outside shell.

What are the spider's main enemies?

Birds, snakes, frogs, lizards, and many other animals. But the foe that spiders fear most is the wasp. This insect stings the spider with a poison that paralyzes but does not kill it. The wasp drags the spider to its nest, then lays an egg on its body. When the egg hatches, the young wasp eats the spider!

Wolf spider

How do spiders stay out of trouble?

Most are very small and can hide easily. Also, many have colors or markings that let them blend in with their surroundings. Some spiders look like leaves—green to match living leaves, brown to match dead leaves. Lichen spiders seem to disappear on tree trunks because they resemble bark. Crab spiders slowly change color to match the flower they sit on. A few crab spiders look like bird droppings. No one wants to eat them!

Long-jawed orb weaver

Jumping spider

Green lynx spider

Huntsman spider

How do tarantulas defend themselves?

By shooting out hairs. A tarantula uses its legs to brush hairs off its body and into the eyes and mouth of an attacker. The sharp, hooked hairs sting and hurt the enemy, giving the tarantula time to scamper away. Small wonder that most would-be attackers leave tarantulas alone!

What happens when an enemy bites off a spider's leg?

If the spider is young, it grows a new one. But most kinds of spiders lose this ability as they get older.

Some spiders know just what to do when under attack. They break off one of their own eight legs. Then they run away at top speed on the remaining seven. Strange to say, the broken leg twitches and wriggles as soon as it breaks off. How confusing this must be for the spider's enemy!

Crab spider

Wolf spider

How do male spiders court females?

Carefully. That's because female spiders are almost always bigger and stronger than males. What's more, the females often eat their mates!

Males attract females in various ways. Some shake the silky threads of a web to lure a female and then stroke her body with their legs. Others wave their legs about to catch the eye of a female. Still others make "friendly" sounds as part of their courting.

How many eggs does a female spider lay?

An average of about 100 at a time. The actual numbers range from 1 or 2 for tiny spiders up to 3,000 eggs for very large ones.

Where do females lay their eggs?

On a layer of silk that they spin. The females then cover the eggs with another layer of silk. This forms a holder for the eggs called an egg sac.

Many female spiders lay their eggs and then leave. Others care for their eggs. Some spiders set the egg sac in a burrow they have dug in the ground. Others place it in a web, attach it to a leaf or plant, or hide it under a log, rock, or pile of dead leaves. Female wolf spiders carry the egg sac around with them until the eggs hatch!

What happens when the eggs hatch?

Tiny baby spiders, called spiderlings, are born. In some cases, the females feed and protect the young. A mother huntsman spider, for example, spits up digested food for her spiderlings to eat.

Many spiderlings are on their own right from the start. Web spinners can build their own webs soon after they hatch. Others must hunt for food. If there's not enough food for everyone, spiderlings sometimes eat one another!

Wolf spider
with egg sac

Wolf spider with spiderlings

What helps spiderlings find homes?

The wind. Right after hatching, each spiderling runs up to the top of a plant with its dragline. Any light breeze lifts the dragline and spider like a kite or a balloon on a windy day.

Depending on the wind, the small spider can stay aloft for weeks. But finally it falls to earth and makes a home of its own—with little danger of overcrowding!

What happens as spiders grow bigger?

They molt, or shed their old skin. As the spider's body grows in size, it wiggles out of its stiff outer shell, called an exoskeleton. The spider then grows a new shell. Young spiders molt as many as 13 times before they become mature.

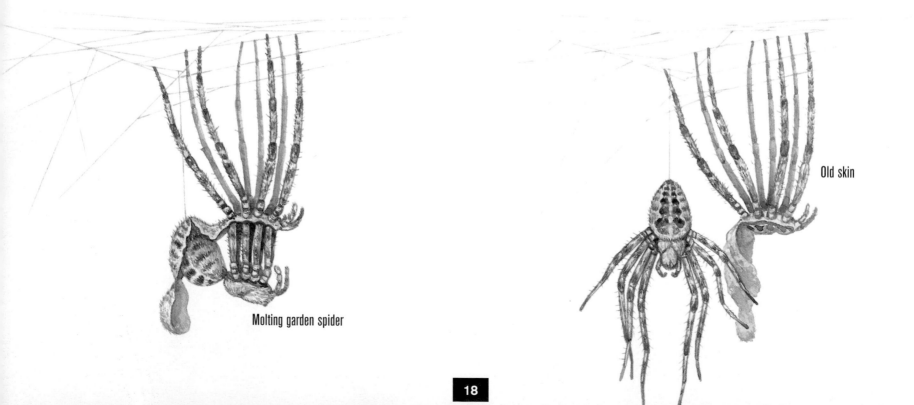

Molting garden spider

Old skin

How long do spiders live?

It varies. Many live only one year. Wolf spiders live several years. Tarantulas are the longest-lived. Scientists think some tarantulas reach the ripe old age of 20 years.

Where do spiders live?

Everywhere on Earth, except around the South Pole. Spiders live indoors and out, on mountaintops and in water, in warm places mostly, but also where it is cold.

Molting tarantula

WEB SPINNERS

How does a garden spider spin a web?

Step by step. The spider:

1. presses its spinnerets against a twig or a blade of grass. It forces out some liquid silk and moves away, drawing out the sticky thread.
2. either carries the thread and attaches it to another object or lets the breeze do the job.
3. walks back and forth along this bridge line, adding silk to make it stronger and tighter.
4. spins a long, drooping thread between the two ends of the bridge line.
5. drops a thread from the middle of the sagging line to the ground, which forms a letter Y.
6. spins threads from the center of the Y out to the edges, making them look like the spokes of a bicycle wheel.
7. covers the spokes with a long, dry spiral to strengthen the web.
8. finishes the web by spinning a spiral of sticky silk on top of the first spiral.

This kind of web is called an orb web. It takes less than an hour to build.

How do orb weavers catch their prey?

They stay still and wait. The spider hangs head-down in the center of the web with its feet on the threads. When an insect is caught, the spider feels the vibrations with its feet. The spider rushes out. It sinks its poisonous fangs into the struggling victim. The spider ties up the insect with sticky silk like a little mummy. Only then does the spider eat the bug.

Orb web construction

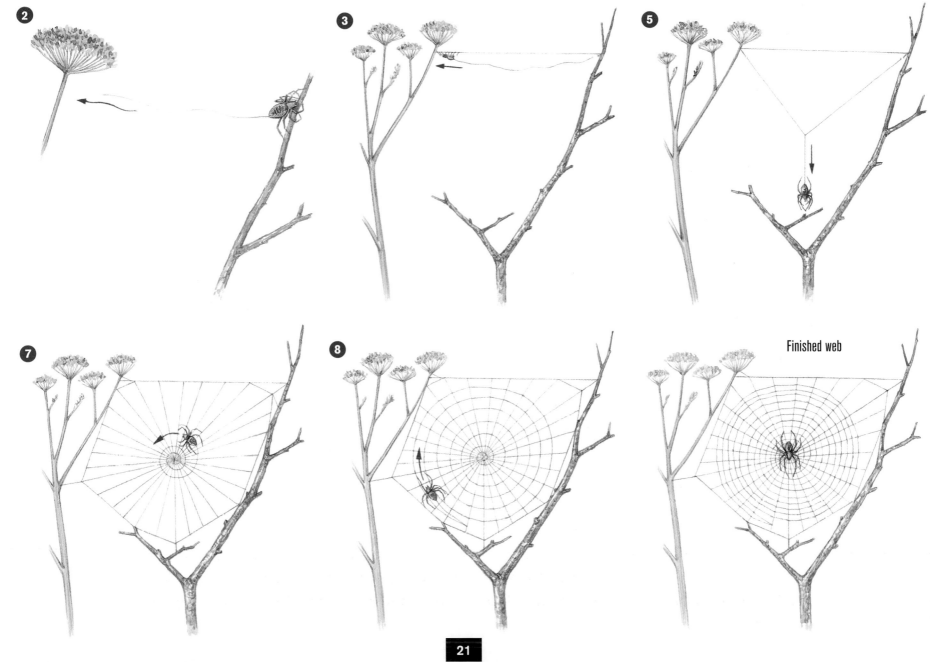

Finished web

Funnel web

Grass spider

Do all spiders wait in the center of the web?

No. Some wait off to the side. Others leave the web, but hold on to a silk line attached to the web's center. But no matter where they sit, the spiders can feel the web threads vibrate when an insect is caught. And they know just what to do next.

What is the most common kind of web?

The tangled web. This web is a loosely woven jumble of silk threads. House spiders spin tangled webs in dark, quiet corners in people's homes. You can find their webs attached to walls, ceilings, windows, lights and lamps, and other surfaces.

The web's threads are long and sticky. The spider that spins a tangled web usually lives at the edge of the web.

Which spider builds large webs in tall grass?

The grass spider. The web is shaped like a funnel. It has a wide, flat sheet on top that gets thinner as it reaches down to the ground.

The grass spider hides at the bottom of the funnel web. Sometimes only its front feet can be seen. But when an insect lands on the sheet, the spider scoots out and strikes.

Which spider makes a sheetlike web?

The hammock spider. This spider spins a flat web that hangs like a cloud between blades of grass or branches of trees or shrubs. Above the web the spider spins a tangle of separate silk threads. Then the spider sits and waits.

Insects often crash into the hard-to-see tangle of silk threads. Bang! They're knocked down into the sheetlike web below. And before you know it, the spider is enjoying its tasty meal.

Which spider becomes part of its own web?

The triangle spider. The spider first attaches two points of its web to two twigs. It then grasps the third point with its front legs while using its back legs to hold on to a silken anchor on another twig.

When an insect strikes the web, the triangle spider loosens the end it holds. The web springs forward, pulling the insect inside. As the insect struggles, it gets tangled up even more. The triangle spider covers the insect with silk and carries it back to a corner of the web. Eating a large insect can take the triangle spider a whole day!

Which spider makes the simplest web of all?

The episinus spider. The web consists of two sticky threads that hang down from a low branch and are attached to the ground. The lower parts are covered with drops of sticky silk glue. The spider hangs down, holding the threads apart with its legs. Any insect that bumps into one of the threads gets stuck. Its movements knock the thread free of the ground. As the thread curls up, it raises the insect to the waiting spider.

Does any spider carry its web with it?

The net-casting, or web-throwing, spider. Between its legs, this spider spins a rubbery web the size of a postage stamp. Then it hangs down from a low branch with its head just above the ground and waits for prey to pass by. Sooner or later, the spider spots a likely victim. It stretches out the web and slams it down over the insect, wrapping it up like a bug in a rug!

Do spiders ever build webs together?

Yes. Groups of hundreds or thousands of social spiders sometimes come together to weave a gigantic web. Some larger ones, such as the eresid social spider, can cover an entire tree.

Social spider webs

SPIDERS THAT HUNT

What do hunting spiders look like?

They tend to have long, round bodies and big, strong jaws. Also, their legs are longer and thicker than those of web-spinning spiders. Spiders that hunt depend on strength and speed, not webs, to capture their prey.

How do hunters catch insects?

By surprise attack. Some lie in wait for their prey. These spiders hide in burrows or silken tubes until insects come to them. Others wander about, searching for creatures that would make a good meal. When they find their prey, they rush in for the kill.

When do spiders hunt?

Mostly at night. During the day you can find them hiding under leaves, beneath rocks, or behind peeling bark.

Still, some spiders do hunt during the day. You sometimes see them running around in the bright sun, chasing insects that come within striking distance.

Do hunting spiders have good sight?

Yes and no. Daylight hunters usually can see very well—especially straight ahead. Most also have a second pair of eyes that look up, giving them even better vision. But spiders that hunt in the dark usually depend on other senses to find and capture their prey. Despite their large eyes, most are quite nearsighted.

Huntsman spider

Huntsman spider

Which are the largest hunting spiders?

Tarantulas. With their legs stretched out, these hairy spiders can be as big as dinner plates—10 inches (25 cm) across!

Where do tarantulas make their homes?

In underground burrows. To make its home, the tarantula digs out bits of earth with its powerful jaws. It forms the soil into balls and carries them away. Then it waterproofs the walls of its burrow with a mixture of soil and saliva. Finally, the tarantula carefully lines the burrow with silk.

Most burrows are small and comfy, but they can become very tight if the spider tries to turn around!

Tarantula

How do tarantulas surprise their prey?

They wait until an insect or small animal comes within range. Then the spider rears up and slams its two large fangs down on the victim, delivering a deadly shot of poison. The tarantula holds on to its prey until the poison starts to work.

Tarantulas mostly hunt beetles, grasshoppers, and other insects. But a large tarantula can make a meal of a small frog, mouse, snake, lizard, or even a bird—if it can catch one.

Are tarantulas brave hunters?

No. Most tarantulas are fearful. They stay in their burrows until the sun sets. Then they creep out to find something to eat. But they never go too far. If anything scares them, they dart back inside.

How can you tell if a tarantula is in its burrow?

Look at the opening. If the burrow is open, the spider is probably out hunting. In the morning, after a night's hunt, the tarantula usually spins a web to cover the burrow entrance. A covered burrow tells you the spider is most likely at home.

Which other spiders live in burrows?

Trapdoor spiders. They actually build a trapdoor, or lid, of silk, soil, and spit, over the burrow entrance. The trapdoor hides the burrow from enemies. It also protects the spider while it is inside.

Trapdoor spiders don't move around much. At night, they raise the trapdoor enough to stick out their front legs and look for passing insects. If they find one, they lunge out, grab it, and drag the bug down into the burrow for a nice, quiet meal.

Can insects sneak past the burrow of a trapdoor spider?

Not easily. Some trapdoor spiders spin silk threads called trip wires. The threads stretch out from the burrow like the spokes of a wheel. If an insect stumbles on a trip wire, the hunter feels the thread shake. This signals the spider to spring out, find the bug, and capture it. Pretty tricky!

Which hunting spider lives in a silk tube?

The purse-web spider. This spider spends its whole life inside a silken purse. The purse is shaped like a tube about 10 inches (25 cm) long and ³/₄ inch (2 cm) wide. The spider places the lower part of the tube inside its sloping burrow and the upper part on the ground or along the trunk of a tree. Once inside, the spider seals both ends of the tube. Look as hard as you can. You won't find the entrance or exit.

How does the purse-web spider hunt?

It waits for an insect to cross the outside part of the tube. As soon as the purse-web spider feels the vibrations, it darts to the spot and bites the insect *right through the silk tube*! Its fangs pierce the insect's soft belly. The purse-web spider then drags the dead insect into its burrow. But before enjoying its meal, the spider repairs the hole in the purse!

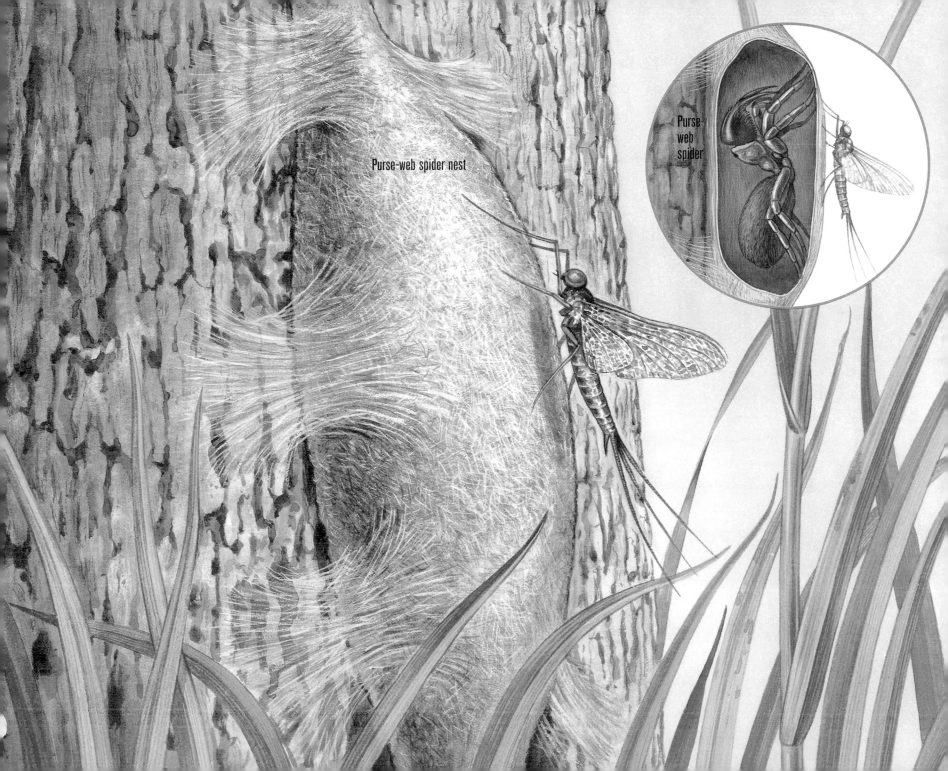

Purse-web spider nest

Purse-
web
spider

Which other spiders lie in wait for their prey?

Crab spiders. These spiders look just like crabs with their short, wide, flat bodies. They also walk sideways and backward like crabs.

Crab spiders usually sit very still on a flower, their two powerful front legs ready to grasp any insect that comes too close. One poisonous bite is enough to kill an insect quickly—even one that is several times the spider's size.

On which insects do crab spiders prey?

Bees, butterflies, and other flower visitors. Since crab spiders are often the same color as the flowers they sit in, their victims can't see them—until it's too late.

Which spiders are the best hunters?

Wolf spiders. These spiders don't wait for their victims to come to them. They wander about in search of their prey.

Do wolf spiders hunt in packs like real wolves?

No, they usually hunt alone. But wolf spiders are swift runners and chase their quarry just as wolves do. When they get close, wolf spiders put on a burst of speed and leap onto their victims. Very few insects are able to fight off fierce wolf spider attacks.

Goldenrod spider,
a kind of crab spider

Which are the most colorful hunting spiders?

Jumping spiders. Their bodies are covered with brightly colored hair or scales. Each kind has its own special markings. The males also have small spines and hairs that decorate their legs.

Do jumping spiders really jump?

They sure do—and far. This tiny spider is seldom more than $1/2$ inch (1.3 cm) long. Yet it can leap about 40 times its own length to land on a fly, bug, or beetle. If you could jump as well for your size, you'd cover twice the length of a basketball court in a single giant leap!

Like other spiders, jumping spiders trail silken draglines behind them. They fasten the safety line before they pounce—and away they go!

How do jumping spiders catch their prey?

They stalk them. When the jumping spider gets close, it pounces like a cat hunting a mouse. Nine times out of ten it lands right on the money!

Jumping spider

Jumping spiders

Do any spiders live near water?

Yes. Fisher spiders prey mainly on insects that fall into ponds, pools, marshes, or swamps. These large spiders sit on banks or water plants, with their front legs in the water. As soon as they pick up the vibrations of any insects on the surface, the fisher spiders scurry across the water to the spot. Their light bodies let them run on top of the water—without even getting wet! They snatch their prey in their strong jaws and head to shore to eat in peace.

Do any spiders go fishing?

Yes, fisher and swamp spiders do. They sit and wiggle their legs in the water until they attract a small fish or tadpole. Then, in a flash, the spider sinks its poisonous fangs into the animal and plucks it out of the water.

The Mexican fishing spider attaches itself to a leaf and floats across a pond as if on a raft. From here, the spider hunts its prey.

Fisher spider

Which spider can breathe underwater?

The water spider. Even though it looks like an ordinary spider, the water spider can swim and dive, while other spiders can't.

This spider spins a bell-shaped web that it attaches to an underwater plant. Then it rises to the surface. It wiggles its legs to trap a bubble of air against its body, carries the bubble down to its web, and releases it into the web. The spider keeps on trapping and releasing the bubbles until the web has an air bubble big enough to hold the spider.

How does the water spider find food?

It hunts. The water spider usually stays in its underwater house with its long legs sticking out. As soon as a small creature swims by, the spider strikes, drags it back into the air bubble, and then starts its meal.

Water spider ready to add air to its web

Bolas spiders

How do bolas spiders hunt?

With a glob of sticky silk at the end of a long thread. Bolas spiders use the glue ball the way cowboys use lassos. The spiders twirl the ball in the air and fling it at a flying moth, their favorite food. Once the insect is stuck on the glue ball, the bolas spider pulls in the thread and devours the moth.

Some African bolas spiders keep whirling their gluey thread through the air all the time. They're always ready to hurl it at a passing insect.

Bolas spiders sometimes wait a long time for a catch. But after about 15 minutes, the sticky silk dries out and loses its gumminess. So the spider pulls in the line, eats the glob at the end, and makes another one.

Which spiders have the worst manners?

Spitting spiders. When an insect comes within range, they fire two zigzag lines of sticky goo through their fangs. This glues the insect to the spot. The spitting spider then has plenty of time to kill and eat the stuck bug.

What is a banana spider's favorite food?

Not bananas, as you might think. A banana spider hunts cockroaches and other insects. The spider's name comes from its habit of hitching rides on bunches of bananas!

Bolas spider

LIVING WITH SPIDERS

How many spiders live around your house?

Lots. A scientist once studied a 1 acre (0.4 ha) meadow near Washington, D.C., and found about 64,000 spiders living there!

What is a cobweb?

An old, tangled spiderweb that has collected dust and dirt. Sometimes the cobweb is just a bunch of draglines that spiders no longer use.

Do spiders bite people?

Hardly ever. While many people fear spiders, most spiders are very shy. Spiders either stand still or run away when someone comes close. Only in rare cases will a spider bite a person who bothers it. Although spiders are poisonous, the poison is usually too weak to hurt humans. Also, spider fangs are usually too short to break a person's skin.

Which spider is most dangerous to humans?

The black widow. The poison of this small, shiny-black spider with red hourglass markings is 15 times more powerful than rattlesnake poison!

Black widows are dangerous because they often live close to humans—in piles of trash, woodpiles, the lids of garbage cans, and other places around the house. If someone presses bare skin against a black widow, there's a chance the spider will bite in self-defense. But the good news is that a black widow bite almost never kills a person.

Brown recluse spider

Are there other dangerous spiders?

Yes, brown recluse spiders, which are also called violin spiders because of the marks on their bodies. The bite of the brown recluse doesn't kill people, but its fangs may leave a deep wound 6 inches (15 cm) wide that takes up to four months to heal.

Which is the toughest of all spiders?

The Brazilian wandering spider. People can't scare it away. The harder you try to hit it, the harder it tries to bite! This spider often hides in people's homes and sometimes has been known to give a deadly bite.

When did a spider help win a war?

In the year 1306. Robert the Bruce, King of Scotland, was at war with England. Once, after losing six battles in a row, the king hid out in a barn. While there, he noticed a spider trying to swing on a thread from one beam to another. Six times he saw the spider try, missing the beam every time. But finally, on the seventh try, the spider succeeded.

Inspired by the spider, King Robert came out of hiding and returned to his troops. This time he won and was able to drive the English out of Scotland.

Can spiders change your luck?

Some people believe so. In nineteenth-century America, people hung a nutshell with a spider inside around their necks to ward off disease. In Polynesia, they say you reach heaven by climbing a giant ladder of spider silk! Even today, some people think you will have good luck if you save or protect a spider. As the old poem puts it:

If you wish to live and thrive,
Let a spider run alive.

How do spiders help people?

They eat insect pests. In California, wolf spiders prey on the aster leafhopper, which destroys rice crops. In the Fiji Islands, jumping spiders control the caterpillars that kill coconut palm trees. Other spiders keep pests such as cotton worms, gypsy moths, and pea aphids in check.

Crab spiders are perhaps most helpful. In 1923, they put an end to a plague of bedbugs that struck Athens, Greece. Each spider ate 30 or 40 bedbugs a day! Relatives of this spider live in warehouses today, preying on the pests that ruin stored foods.

Where do people catch fish with spiderwebs?

On islands in the South Pacific. In New Guinea, for example, some people use the huge, tough webs of wood spiders as ready-made fishing nets. The nets are 6 feet (2 m) wide and strong enough to catch fish that weigh as much as 1 pound (0.5 kg).

Which famous doctor prescribed spiders?

Dr. Thomas Muffet, around 1600. Today, people remember Dr. Muffet best as the father of Patience Muffet, the real Little Miss Muffet of the nursery rhyme:

Little Miss Muffet
Sat on a tuffet
Eating her curds and whey.
Along came a spider
Who sat down beside her
And frightened Miss Muffet away.

When she got sick, her father probably gave her mashed spiders—just as he did for other patients. No wonder Miss Muffet ran away from the spider!

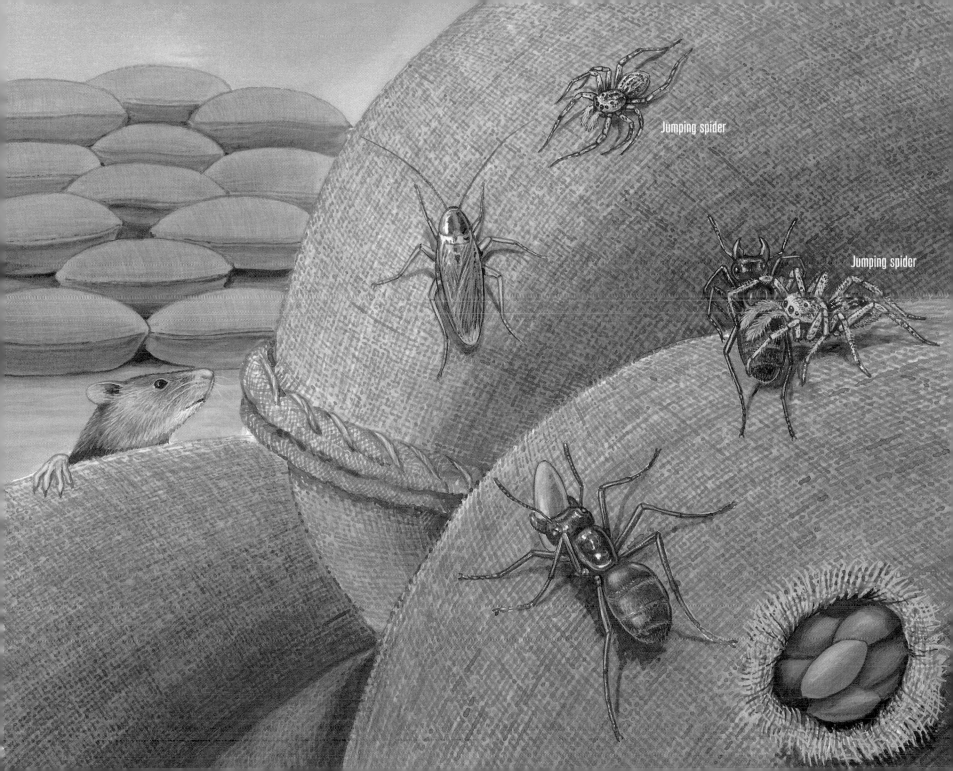

Jumping spider

Jumping spider

Can I collect webs?

Yes. You'll need talcum powder, a sheet of black or dark construction paper, and a can of spray adhesive.

Look for a fresh web on a plant or bush or near a door or window. **Be sure the web has no spider on or near it.** Gently sprinkle some talcum powder on the web to outline the threads. Then use two hands to hold the paper flat behind the web. Slowly and carefully lift the paper into the web, so that it sticks to the paper.

Place the paper with the web against a tree or other surface. Spray the paper lightly with the adhesive and let it dry. Now hang it in a frame or place it in a folder.

Are spiders important to life on Earth?

Certainly! Spiders feed on flies that carry disease, bees that sting, mosquitoes that bite, moths that make holes in clothes, and all the insect pests that destroy crops and stored foods.

At the same time, spiders are food for frogs, lizards, fish, birds, and even skunks and shrews. Without spiders, many living beings might not have enough to eat.

How can I help spiders?

Here are a few things you can do:

- Plant trees and shrubs to attract spiders.
- Leave some leaves, stones, and logs around your yard as hiding places for spiders.
- Do not harm spiders you catch. Put them back after you study them.
- Do not use insect sprays that also kill spiders and useful insects.
- Join a nature group and work to save spiders that are in danger of disappearing from rain forests and from your neighborhood, too.

INDEX

About the Authors

The authors happily share their home with many spider visitors, whenever they come to call. "We welcome them," the Bergers say, "because most spiders are harmless and do a great job of killing flies and other insects that carry diseases."

About the Illustrator

Roberto Osti says that in order to paint the spiders in this book, he entered the hidden world of these ingenious predators. "It was fun, like a backyard safari," he says, "and I had to think and see like a spider."